FINISHING LINE PRESS

www.finishinglinepress.com

The Tree Surgeon
Dreams of Bowling

poems by

Jayne Marek

Finishing Line Press
Georgetown, Kentucky

The Tree Surgeon
Dreams of Bowling

ACKNOWLEDGMENTS
The author thanks the editors of the following publications in which the following poems,
or versions thereof, previously appeared:

About Place Journal: "Drowned Mole"
Apogee [Franklin, IN]: "Cut Glass," "Harpers Ferry," "Trees in Memory"
Blast Furnace: "Mistakes"
Central American Literary Review: "Waves"
Cincinnati Writers Project Anthology 2012—A Few Good Words: "The Tree Surgeon
      Dreams of Bowling"
Flying Island: "Two Variations (for Hazel)"
Gyroscope Review: "Carp Mobile," "For Roger"
In and Out of Rough Water: "The Tree Surgeon Dreams of Bowling"
Notre Dame Review 43 (Winter 2017): "Chances," "Cloud Solid," "Her Feet," "Moon Jellies"
Panoply: "Con Trail"
Peacock Journal: "Buddha Touch," "Grass Writing," "Hands in Temple Smoke," "Nishijin
      Textile Center, Kyoto," "The Wood Turner's Shop, Itsukushima"
Saxifrage: "Spring Cleaning"
Sin Fronteras / Writers Without Borders: "Burntcoat Head"
Tipton Poetry Journal: "Prognosis"
Washington 129 Digital Chapbook Project: "The Ferry at Six-Thirty, Dark,"
Women's Studies Quarterly: "Postcard from Assam"

Publisher: Leah Maines

Editor: Christen Kincaid

Cover Art: Jayne Marek

Author Photo: Lylanne Musselman

Cover Design: Elizabeth Maines McCleavy

Printed in the USA on acid-free paper.
Order online: www.finishinglinepress.com
      also available on amazon.com

Author inquiries and mail orders:
Finishing Line Press
P. O. Box 1626
Georgetown, Kentucky 40324
U. S. A.

Table of Contents

III: Of Grace

About the Author

To Joe
and all our loved ones

I: Just Out of Reach

Prognosis

Raking and raking,
But the long tines cannot gather up grief
That waits beyond the fence.

Grief is like fear
Seen from another direction. The two hunch over,
Stare like stone monsters guarding a stoop.

The lion-dog of fear is agape with fangs.
The lion-dog of grief grips the pearl of the world
With suffocating claws.

I rake the wet lawn, flattening it
In one direction. It will stay that way
Through several more rains.

Even when I go inside
I know the shapes are out there.
Even in darkness.

I remember the cries made by rake tines
As they scarred the fence,
Unable to clear out the fallen

Leaves, the soaked moss,
Broken sticks
Left by the storm.

Mistakes

Mistakes are fire and ice, ice and river—
What the sages say about burn and winter.
I'm unable to do over or find shelter.

I will expire with regrets whenever
My life blows up in a stained-glass shatter,
Shards of color broken, never

To be repaired. What's lost, I haven't found.
I have erred
Repeatedly, lacerated

My skin with the sharpened
Edges of my own tongue's words,
The frozen roughness loosened

By torrents beneath until it splits.
Sad, wishing to not have said this
Or that, to pull back the dark flag passing between lips,

Not unstoppable, just let slip.
Tell me again the tale of no forgiveness. It's
Hard ground, the meager comfort of precise breaks.

Drowned Mole

At the side of the path, you lie fat as a lost sock. Lobed toes spread in surprise as you entered the light that was your darkest burrow. A handful of slate gray, your fur sleek as a rich matron's coat on opening night. Sheen of stars across it, a galaxy of sand. Forced from the tight channel of earth that pulsed with water, the throat of a whale. The god of moles, humble and significant. Forgive this stick that lifts you at ribs and hips. I love your defenseless tummy, turned up, no longer pleading. Your nose, chill-blanched, splays like tendrils of a spring flower. It is morning, pink, a slightly bared gum.

Moon Jellies

transfixed by water's transformation from darkness
I watch jellyfish tentacles trail lazily
in this aquarium tank

a translucent wake
pulses with poisonous attraction
as dangerous as a mind set loose

footless   handless   unable to rest
its mouth of pink pulp   silent
about what humans ache to learn

the jelly fades to blue   others float into focus
the pumps of their bodies heartless
they bumble against each other slowly

as if drifting meant nothing   indecision
a turn in darkness toward an inaccessible shape
the purpose of lives   mine

theirs   yours   flowing glass seized into stillness
shows us each other
gorgeous   made of lethal matter

Fable

Here is what you'll remember, old man, old woman,
who pine for a story that says life is simple
as this scalped green yard,
smooth as sodded graves, this bare subdivision
bunkered by curbs along streets named for trees
now choked gray, or felled,

years ago. A flurry of wings
on the gravel, one crow flat on its back,
two that hold it down, bob in rhythm, stab in turns
between their spread claws. Each pierce
of a beak brings a squeal, a kick from the held crow's
raised claws. If you stop

to watch, unsure whether the car window
frames something real, perhaps you will lift
one hand until the tormentors
pause from pecking the helpless one,
turn their wild heads
to look at you.

Clay

A leathery clay pot swings from her hand
as she approaches. She is shadow, covers half the sky.
Tall, heavy in the middle like the vases she pulls,
kicking that wheel to hell back in the barn.
Firm grip of her fingers pinching clay, shoulders,
ears, bean blossoms. Beans burst fat as slugs.
Tomatoes try to please her, lean over,
red globes pulling down the greens. Her green pot
is going to the kiln, masonry box that seethes
in the back yard amid a footing of pebbles.
She is of stones, of heat so intense
she cooks beans for hours, forgets their gray slime
on the stove. Fresh tomato seeds dribble
down a chin, that's all there is. Overcooked bean slop
flies into the barnyard. At a distance
her shoulders hunch over the kiln, tongs wave.
Stay back. It was Walter, with a silver burn scar
on his neck she identifies after he's pulled from the creek
in spring. She dunks pots in that creek,
keeps dragging steaming racks down the slope
where brush is raggedly cut in one spot. Never glazes them,
stacks them on shelves along one barn wall
to gather cobwebs. Her apron's as old as the weeds.
She never tires of scoring the clay's flesh in new ways.

The Deepest Snow

That was the deepest I ever went into the snow.
—Naomi Shihab Nye

1.

The deepest? Up to my neck,
alone amid pine trees at a ski station
at the end of a metro line north
of Oslo in January,
the cliché of cold and snowiness one would predict.
I was breaking trail and lost my balance,
remember the wet shock of snow down my collar,
my legs splayed on a drift as if across a sofa,
tipped against heavy lumps—
I might not be able to get up.
The place was so lovely,
deeply folded, white and black,
remote as an owl's lair
and harsh, as if under the owl's eyes.

2.

But that was still snow, quiet snow,
having settled across land.
Flying snow? In my face?
I recall confusion and shouting,
a telephone held away from my ear
the last time my former best friend and I ever spoke,
everything slippery and grayish white—
or perhaps
the gales of dementia that blew into a life
more heavily than anyone expected
even though the clouds,
when they lined the horizon,
looked bleak;
no one could take the warnings
this seriously.

Cut Glass

On a windowsill, a pale mouth
of distortion
is the goblet
in mid-winter, rime on its lip

behind the heavy drapery drawn
against deep cold
endless as overcast sky

I had forgotten
one amid the others, and winter
froze the crystal in place
a thin bowl fogged with false breath

now white drops shake from
the lifted stem
cracked from the base
by forgetfulness worse
than intent

Winter Runes

This snow will stop
as it began.
Now wind rises to speak.

A young sparrow, left behind,
utters a sharp cry
over and over.

Black seeds fragrant as past summer
fall from my hands.
Everywhere particles of white

gather to hide
narrow tracks where juncos hopped
and shadows where the seeds dived.

Harpers Ferry

A long railroad bridge crosses the river junction,
getting away fast.
Always there is fog
breathing from the brick walls,
naming failure.

In December, cobblestones are fat with cold,
houses nailed shut.
History, an old jacket full of holes,
lets in the screech
of an engine invisible behind mountains.

A visitor looks in vain
for something that is not gray river water
nor the rain blotting sooty chimneys.
But no, the dead
cannot be seen through the windows of time,

smeared over long ago;
all had their chance.
An odor of decay drags its arms across storefronts,
uneven as old teeth
bared to the sleet.

Unknown Pacific

Underwater sounds travel along my bones, trying to keep ahead of the cold front. I lie in hospital sheets, listening to spectral whispers of a pump that reaches into my veins, where the curious catheter floats, amid red poisons in my arm. Beyond this building, small boats roll, ships slide through the mist past Ediz Hook; further out, tankers enter an unknown Pacific Ocean as night extends ahead of them.

No longer what I was, nor in a birth, the thought of death thinkable, hooked as it is to my wrist in the needle-puncture grip of a bird of prey. It waits and is patient, brooding over my nest of half-sleep. Outside the window, deep water turns. Its echo tide will draw an irregular heartbeat along the coast, becoming fainter. The pebbles murmur, doomed to crumble, each tiny rock loving its purple knuckles, its iron streaks soon to be scoured off by sand.

Cloud Solid

from this top-floor hospital room, I could step
onto a staircase of cumulus scuffed
by many feet

I am not sure I will go

I could lean toward chimney flames
that are and are not   will-o-the-wisps
of autumn   I could fall
toward concrete entranceways
empty of visitors   emergencies

the clouds are never still and never part
into them vanishes a swirl of pigeons

one feather falls   ivory and smoke-dark
sailing straight   rising
it twists and loses its loft
spirals gracefully

its black-spot tip flashes three times

just enough Morse code to begin a distress signal
but too far gone to finish

Flying Through the Universe in My Hand

That thudding
robust heartbeat of the machine-god who held me
in magnetic resonance like a hard symphony
tunneling granite underwater
around my guppy frailty,

now gone quiet—

what remains
is this silent film playing on a computer screen,
imagery of my injured hand,
beautiful blue electric tangle—

I fly through its universe, I chase
my palm bones, fingers
transform into channels of light, the aurora borealis
flows, streaming with bubbles, veins and black
tendons and pearls of tissue

my hand that can climb a rock face,
sew on a button, finesse a bicycle brake
and kill me.

All this darkness is my world of flesh.

In the MRI playback, trails gleam
and twine, ghosts soar through a keyhole to heaven,
paths of swifts marking a coming storm
that blows ashore, burgeons into night.

Injury

Habit reaches for a coffee cup, sees its arm in a cast,
pulls back. Habit clatters silverware across the counter, unable to grasp.
Habit's voice chases the strawberries that spill and roll

under a cupboard edge. The new self stands dumbly to one side
remembering what used to be, what was held
in place by illusions of normalcy. Now one cannot grip

a door handle nor hang up a jacket. Sheets of paper scatter
across the floor. No one can hold scissors to cut out newsprint letters
in a plea: *I am being held in a circle of armlessness.*

Habit, awake through all the black and blue night, listens
to the wind touch everything outside without hands.

So Late Winter

Two weeks into spring, finally,
winter begins to forget us

At the visitation with closed casket,
the destroyed father
knows the flames in his mind
and that he is alone

A faceless calf carcass
leans against a rim of snow
receding from a fence

Mud shows the tines of bent forks
now in the flood's wake
of gray weeds

There was a comet
in the western sky for a few nights,
people said, but clouds blocked it

I wanted to see its bright arm
reaching straight out

Two Variations

—for Hazel, 1951-2011

1. Conjunto

When I hear your name, Hazel, it is 1994,
you and I knee-deep in the Colorado River in Austin, Texas,
under the rock hollows at Barton Springs, both of us visitors
who met at the library and don't have swimsuits
to take with us over lunchtime, under the July sun so rabid
we can't stand to eat. We talk and talk,
your Australian accent telling of loneliness
from one continent to the next,
brown water billowing over our toes
like a thousand sentences to be read and written.
At evening, you drive us in your landlords' Datsun
to a cantina where we order tacos and beer, both
at room temperature, because we are here for the conjunto music
you have never heard before. The Mexican quartet
knows everyone sitting at the patched tables
except us, so the men in silver-seamed pants
flourish their fingertips as they play through the favorites,
listeners' feet shifting on soiled hardwood,
the sandals, the tennis shoes, the polished wingtips
of the older man, the red patent pumps of his lady
who leaps up, takes his hand, and the two smooth their dance
across the floor as all heads turn to follow them
and fans slog overhead, shifting scents of cerveza
and lime, green and tangy, over our greedy hands.

2. No Stairway to Heaven

I dream of staircases that end in midair,
steps of gray composition tiles or faded wood, no railings,
where I wait at the abyss
not knowing how to go on.

Awake today, I remember Mexican pottery

with riotous blue and yellow petals painted
in bold strokes, filling the shops of the Texas street
where we browsed—the colors were happiness.

And we watched an old couple in plain street clothes,
in the cantina that summer night,
who danced seamlessly like two halves
of the same soul.

What I want to say is

I hope you had beauty in your mind as your eyes closed, Hazel,
unable to breathe, fearful of taking the empty step,
and remembered the tall young man,
your lover later that humid night,
every touch a streak of searing orange.

For Roger

The ferry, underway, plunges, a hard heavy light-box against void

Somewhere in the night Strait flow strings of photospheres,
plankton and families of sea creatures that flash to each other

A man I passed on the ferry stairs seemed familiar, as tall as you
who have been gone for five years, or six, I forget
since once the dark sea receives a man, all days cease to be counted,

for him, all colors submerge,
he cannot acknowledge a nod or the static announcing embarkation,
the grind of seismic motors will not rouse him

as the lights of the shore let go finger by finger: blurs of red and yellow
like your Hawaiian shirts, splashes of exuberant rainbow fantasies
I'm going to get better

You knew you were dying from drink
you apologized to your son
trying doesn't necessarily work

So low a tide here we hang offshore for many minutes, not arriving,
unseen water moves like years while we are still

There are so few of us aboard
I almost believe we don't exist

Elegiac Unsonnet for My Cat

After the moon eclipsed into burnt blood
It slowly grew back from one spot of white.

Would that the dying could renew themselves,
Beloved friend. I lost you in the cold
Of winter, at the foot of a renewed
Year, in a collapse of snow. Your golden
Eyes stared open, body already tight
With poisoned muscles, on the pillow we
Had shared the prior night, as I lay next
To you, love, trying to ease our fears.
Your last movements shaped your thin back to me.

When morning came, I made the call, the drive.
Your white fur became ashes, cast afloat
Into December wind. That loss, unwound
From memory, flows now, elusive, past
My reach, brighter now, as if you had lived.

Would the Good People Please Stop Dying?

—for CD Wright, 1949-2016

Driving the two-lane road pre-dawn. Thirty-seven miles per hour. Scraps of frost, the flickering center line. Through mist, an apparition, a lamp, a living room's green walls. Silhouette of a man seated. Still as an oak, he faces the window. Look out, look in. For one second, the seated man and the driver are light and light. Across the road, leafless shadows, a dark saltwater expanse. Stars lap at their own feet. Blacktop like a night ocean tide pulls the car away, its dashboard glowing. Spaceship dials. From one world to another. It happens. If it is not loneliness, then what. Then this.

The Channel Bell

The beautiful garment of life torn by a passing nail,
Torn. Worry pulses through my arms,
Circulating its poison ever nearer to my heart.

The channel bell repeats its lift and fall against waves.
Fall, fall is coming, a season of storms
As the bell counts each loss ahead of time.

Even the shoreline cliffs are young, raw from the claws
Of Pacific weather. Even the cliffs are perishing
As they are made new. How short is a life

Drawn on the sine curve of tides. Wind across wave tops
Takes the clang of the red bell toward a harbor
That driftwood may never reach. I watch from the cliff

As the sea's debris bobs and subsides in its course,
Neither coming nor going. The bell strikes in its cage,
Saying reach, reach for shore,

But the curve of a rocky spit may save you
Or smash you. The voice of the bell tells, in how very few hours
The sea will take everything back.

II: Pacific Rim

Hands in Temple Smoke

At this temple in Tokyo
tucked between concrete walls,
the plank steps sag
dark and winter-stained,
the roof shunts rain down rounded tiles
and stray flower stalks twitch
in the gutters. A woman
in a green raincoat
comes to the temple door,
bows with eyes closed
at the wide black pot on a pedestal
where thin candles burn in sand.
Late afternoon.

Boys and girls with bookbags
and blue uniforms
stride past in twos and threes,
gray riders pass
on bicycles heavy with sacks.
Crows bob to their own coarse cries.

The woman reaches into the bitter wisps
of silver and white, waves them
toward her face, her heart.
She enters the building
that breathes of old wood
and dust, the sting of purifying smoke
light as a scarf
across her shoulders.

Buddha Touch

Finches flit in the depths
of this temple, stir
on the rafters.

I stand in the chill
and reach to pat your cheek
as my fingers tremble

with age, with toothache,
my silent tongue a lotus.
Beatific one,

hand raised as if
you would touch me too,
a halo of incense

envelops us both. I wait
to rise in your thoughts,
lift with you on the clouds.

Panda Mania

At the Ueno zoo shop in Tokyo
black and white
ranks of panda toys sit
at child's-eye level

To the left, half the toys
have pink ribbons on their necks
To the right, the other half
tied in blue

Oh for more pandas,
the whole world thinks

The animals themselves
on this day waddle
toward the bamboo stalks near their fence
ten deep with onlookers

One panda sits back and balances
a bamboo shaft with hind paws
stuffs leaves in its mouth
a tooth gleaming for the cameras

Children wear
panda shoes
panda hats—
a panda logo

on the back of a tiny jacket
is captioned
"Panda Mania"—
the boy stares up at me

until his parents turn and call
and he runs paddle-footed to them

Outside the zoo gates

one vendor features
filled sponge cakes
in that familiar outline

The cook spills batter
into a long silver mold
slides it over coals
watches the gathered children

for a long count
then opens the frames
and flips golden panda shapes
into paper cones

A cloud of sweet smells
brings visitors from a nearby temple
for panda worship
Even the fortune-teller

looks up
and smiles

The Wood Turner's Shop, Itsukushima

Framed by picture windows, the wooden flasks stand
in a harmony of browns and tans, shoulders nearly touching,
ranked like dolls of graduated heights, some with a cup
for a cap, others plain as tumblers, each singular in its beauty
like koi floating in a glassy world of winter chill.

A poem would walk into the shop, under the yellow fabric draped
as a charm over the front door, wide open in January,
would see a dog with curled tail, a woman on a stool.
Light grazes the smooth wooden shapes. The poem tests their dense
heaviness in one hand. The fragrance of good wood, cut

and oiled, darkens the shop corners at mid-afternoon.
I do not speak Japanese, so the poem must smile and nod
to the woman, who indicates these are her husband's works.
The dog stares at her, ignores my extended hand. Shelves
at the rear of the shop—all glass—open to a private garden

with waterfall and dense greenery. The one that I wait for
takes its time amid its fellows, rounded like Buddha figures
in twilight: small globes with raised tips,
lidded bowl like a turtle swimming at the surface,
cylinders with grain-streaks perfectly aligned,

and one with peg cap and double shoulders, the one for me.
A poem observes the gentle movements of hands and paper,
the money, the wrapping with delicacy. Turning to go
and noticing light leaves of rain falling, I nod, yes,
winter in rainy country, which helps everything grow.

Nishijin Textile Center, Kyoto

At a low table, a painter kneels,
head bent, his gaze
leading the tip of his brush
across green cotton.
A swath of soft wax spreads
like the tail of a pheasant
in ghostly mist.
Another man in navy-blue kimono
tucks tiny knobs with a pick,
crinkles thin fabric to a point,
makes knot after knot.
On the remnants table,
red shibori cloth scatters its stars
of undyed specks,
and a silk scene
of women's faces under conical hats
slips between my fingers.
At one end of the sales floor,
the massive poles of wooden looms
carry strips of folded cardboard punched
with the complex codes
of kimono patterns. A rack
of finished robes
rubs delicate sleeves together,
the kimonos whisper
to themselves about me,
gaijin, visitor, my round
and covetous eyes.

Grass Writing

Few people understand this delicate Japanese script
    of ancient words carved
        on a new granite slab.

Notice how the brushstrokes release themselves,
    how the incised poem unbraids its hair,
        lets wind lift its hems.

Two golden maple leaves cling
    to that gray surface,
        trifold shapes rhyming

as if the poet herself
    stroked those leaves with afternoon rain
        and placed them there.

No spoiled deer has nibbled the leaves.
    No one translates these graceful phrases
        that mark the path to a shrine,

they are not hiragana, the old character set,
    they scroll like paths of snails in a garden
        tended for thousands of years

or like reeds undulating in pond shallows
    that a pine-tree trimmer
        leans from his ladder to watch.

In the rain, in winter, in Nara,
    a place of homage,
        long bell-pulls sway

from black rooflines, reach toward wet cobbles,
    lure people to wish—grasp and pull
        the tails of gods' robes,

roll the sounds of iron clappers

over curled roof-tiles
like purifying smoke.

Weeds in the gutters grow without knowing how.
The grass writing on its stone marker
cannot be told.

The Art of Teeth

Outdoors the night rains
    over Japan's haunted past
& a spectator alone
    in a Tokyo museum hall
        shivers

near a Noh mask of a girl with black teeth
    her lips barely parted
a smile part sorrow
    part calculation
        this gaze cannot be broken

on the next wall ghosts sift
    through the fangs of a horned mask
        with a face of fire
jealous Hannya
    the same female power

on a silk scroll
a painted tiger tastes the air
    watching small birds in tree branches
golden gaze & muscles seem to shift
        as if candles leapt in a draft

as if one hand of the artist
had slid in delicious fear
    across a living hide
then she lifted the brush
    & before beginning to paint
        narrowed her eyes

Postcard from Assam

—after Agha Shahid Ali's "Postcard from Kashmir"

Assam under the smooth wooden butt
of heat flattens in morning dust,

its ranks of palm trees leaning east,
relentlessly pressed by winds from the west

that exhale orange clouds in endless scarves
too long to wrap up. Airport windows steam,

plastic chairs hold unwelcome visitors,
the floor scuffed with indeterminate borders.

We are pale foreigners; perhaps we need water.
Lift us over plains, over the spice plants

for which the airliners of our escape are named—
tamarind, cinnamon, anise, clove—

dried with breath through clenched teeth.
Our heels are restless, chair legs cannot move,

all watch the clock, look over every detail
of our baggage, the trickles of sweat

on ragged journeys down our necks
bared to the khaki-drab light.

Lotus-Eaters

The air smells of tea, here in the foothills of Punjab, as we drive
The road toward Darjeeling. A plantation of low bushes
Spreads beneath scattered trees with narrow branches
That hover over the plants, filtering sunlight

That steeps a sweet miasma, which we breathe gratefully
After city congestion and dusty plains. Scents of tea
Roll on our tongues, infuse the insides of our mouths,
Perfume our palates, confuse our thirst with hunger,

Lower our eyelids for a few moments as we desire
Another taste, another, from the breeze through the jeep's windows.
We are lotus-eaters of afternoon air in early summer,
Lulled and happy. The road weaves past the plantings

Then turns away, gives a last glimpse of shaded fields
From the vehicle's rear window, the vistas of green and gold
Fading, then hidden by a sudden turn, a shoulder of rock wall
That jerks across our view, jolts us reluctantly awake.

Her Feet

—at Mother Teresa's tomb

A photograph of her feet after her death
frames them, small as a young girl's,
beneath the blanket covering her corpse,
solving the question of how to photograph the dead
discreetly, to respect the dignity
of knowledge only the dead have earned.
For those who cannot let her go, the picture
verifies her at rest, at last,
identifies her as one who suffered
from bent toe joints jutting sideways—
mundane feet of human clay.

Placards of her life attest to her doubts,
the ache to know a real Jesus. He did not
show himself. She walked forward
all her life into the point of that spear.
She became the face and hands of mercy
that her heart wished to know,
bare feet sizzling in the dust of a land
of thirst and poverty
and never saw her mother again.

Now nuns' robes with blue-striped edges
flow in silence past the marble rectangle.
Saffron blossoms and green leaves shift in hot air
that lifts the curtains behind the vigilant nun
who waits at the foot of the tomb.

The Other Ming

The mountains are merciless. On this Ming section of the Great Wall
Summer sun presses its stones against our shoulders.
A long dragon crawls a thousand miles toward the west

On its slow journey, ready to devour everything it passes.
Heat outlines each scale on the dragon's back, every inch
Of it draped over green brocade slopes.

We take each step at an angle and altitude
That hammers in our hearts, on this war-wall
Closing people out and in, the garment of an emperor

Glowing at midday, blue sky lining the arrow slits.
On a narrow landing, we gasp, admire the view:
Endless staircases that twist along rugged land,

The ochre wall topped with far-off people
So small they might have been stitched with feather needles
Or dropped like millet from the beaks of birds.

We turn back to the only path down death-steep stairs,
Trying to keep our balance against the coming fall.

Carp Mobile

each scale rimmed with black around
an array of poppy petals
orange white gold salmon
turning as if in the wind of a green
meadow of pond-weeds

Kite-Flyers

In Kunming's Green Lake Park, flowerbeds
line a pond with its stone bridge where I,
a hatless visitor too warm at midday,
lean on the rail. A push at my elbow, something seethes
in my ear as a taut string reaches

over my shoulder, taps and moves away.
A wrinkled hand extends from a blue sleeve,
holds a wooden dowel that guides the strand,
shivers with tension for three heartbeats
while my eyes follow the line upward

to a leaping kite as big as a man
with arms spread, rapt in the wind,
a rectangle red and yellow as lily petals.
The elderly kite flyer wields the string
two-handed like a fisherman, blurts a word

to another fellow behind us
who wears a harness carrying a broad reel
wound with still more string. He feeds out line
with a gloved hand. The two old men
keep their arms stiff as levers,

keep their balance. The cord near my head
buzzes like a biplane, flexes, straightens
as the huge wild kite negotiates control—
jerking its jagged path along horizons
that ring miles of fields where figures bend,

swinging mattocks, the whole provincial world,
the kite itself tethered to this green heart—
its tension and joy, its vigor in the air
danced by small men nearly pulled off their feet
by that power they love, ignoring everything else.

Coal Spill, Yunnan

In the countryside, traffic slows
around a half-crushed
coal truck and its spilled cargo

of millions of small chunks
that can perhaps be saved
and sent to the furnaces—

through a haze, green flags
snap in the wind
of a roadside gas stop—where

above the road, on a cliff edge,
a lean-to made of metal plates, ropes,
and canvas tarps

the color of debris
shakes in the gusts
from relentless vehicles

that pass what's small and scattered
as if it were nothing.

Blue on Cang Shan

Blue butterfly wings
  shaped like potato leaves
    smooth and lobed

flutter to a branch
  on a steep slope
    of the mountain Cang Shan
  and as I raise

my camera the wings flash
  swallow tails
    flaunting flat bulb-tips
  like nothing I've seen

At this great height
  after a cable-car ride
    that swung over green
  windy pine-fingers

on mountainsides
  spread in echoing gaps—
    the space between
  heaven and human—

into thin air
  scraped by clouds
    I might fall forever

as if flying in a dream
  across peaks of hope

A shadow shape
  the size of a child's hand
    the blue butterfly
  with its dipping flight

seems to beckon
  in the Chinese manner

palm down
  fingers flexing
    to say come this way
  visitor

toward the edge
  following my beauty
    you know you
      want to

III: Of Grace

Burntcoat Head

These still photographs of ochre water
Roiling on the rocks at Burntcoat Head

Put a chill along my arms and neck
As when my jacket did not protect me

From overwhelming foam and spray
When the Bay of Fundy crashed in its bed.

I saw the squall line overtake
Muddy red cliffs and slant meadows

Late in summer, presaging the fury
Of cold seasons almost upon us,

The neatly painted box of the lighthouse
And the quick gold and white flowers

Shuddering in the wind. And I,
A visitor, breathless, was reminded

That edges change, yet remain—frontiers
Are worthwhile to want and find,

Lean into—as if one can learn to stand
Amid these powers and escape. I did.

I wonder whether knowing this matters,
As if what can kill us listens to the mind.

Waves

Western shore. Evening waves
cast the sun in bronze,
weighted water
across our arms,
ocean neither cold nor warm,
our new element,
a marriage.

Time now has shifted the bluffs
that I remember
rose above us, rugged-
knuckled, red—
we were young,
not tired of the struggle
with the tide,

sunset that soaked
the world.
We could not believe
how deeply the color
flowed around us,
how we might never
swim in such a glow again.

The Ferry at Six-Thirty, Dark,

draws up to the dock in cold saltwater, nestles so softly
we don't notice when its movement finesses into sway.
January tides lift and shift the surface; rain holds us
like coats of waterfalls we cannot remove. The car ramp
lowers and settles, its pad-ends waver like lips without words.
Figures with crisscross vests, luminous snowmen, gesture
our vehicles forward one by one until each vanishes,

the florid reflections of departing taillights slide
across wheelhouse windows. Travelers make what we can of this
elusive, mundane folly, enact it again and again, weaving
our lives of gentle tenuous connections.

Chances

He said he couldn't let go of the picture of himself in ruin,
And I fear that I am also in his picture, impossible as that is,
The decades of his death having flown past me lifting the hair of my youth
Until everything was gone except this square of shiny paper
The way photos used to look, black and white with a deckled edge
As if to fancy up the elbow-patched sweaters, felt hats with a dent
Knocked in the crown. My father's hat, that is, on the table to my right
With the ashtray and a dish of olives.

Now I wonder who was visiting our house that evening, because
The walls are dark, the tabletop formica-bright, and someone's arm
Elbows into the snapshot, as if the picture-taker, my mother maybe,
Didn't think too hard about framing people to "tell their story."
I can almost hear the rasp of the shutter and see the blue pop
Of lightbulb that dazzles for a second.

Who was that man? we ask ourselves later as grownup children,
Going through the boxes of photos from the last house my parents lived in,
Stacks of curling 3-1/2" prints, this legacy of figures in the shadows,
Saved as if forever in drawers of the dining room breakfront under shelves
With delicate red pressed-glass cordials offering their toasts of dust
At their brims, waiting for visitors who never come anymore
And who never will have a name but who reached into our lives anyway
And took, took our father's, our mother's attention, took that
And pasted it to these scraps.

Woods Path

Above me, hidden by leaves, kinglets
comment on my unimportance
from the rough heights of Douglas-fir.
A towhee shifts its dry note under a bush
until my steps pass. This trail

pushes through brown weeds
tinged with mold, held by rain
the forest resists and takes
according to its whims, by which things
thrive or wither. One spot may be better

than another; how can one know
what is best, what is death,
what matters? A turn takes me past
old roots reared up, a fallen trunk,
the hollow under its feet filled with mud.

Sweet Spot for Owls

dusk thickens
frigid air
why do we believe
that waiting will work

that winter will feed us
when all around us are
empty ribs of trees

but then a shade
at hip height flickers

a shape the color
of weeds in near-darkness
that ghost of hope

silent
and we are still

listening for a mouse-
rustle of possibility
watching for the
clutch of the night-glove

Heron in Puget Sound

A gray shadow above shadow,
a boat shape sailing below itself
floats on water dark as loss.

Long neck feathers into dusk.
It leans into listening, waits
while onshore the pines grow

a needle's width. The heron
with hesitant step glides
forward toward a pier,

its legs hinge-deep in the silk
scarf of water, a white fringe
of surf. Its caution,

its concentration.
Lightless, a cargo ship becomes
a distant hill. The heron's

jointed leg
poses in mid-step,
headland and point black to the brink.

My shape may mean
danger. The heron steps to
the edge of sight.

A fish spine of cloud
will disintegrate in an hour,
and a board in the dock

has worn loose, leaving
a rusty scab, a nail pointing: a spell—
shadow and cloud and ship hover.

I wish not to be

broken again by cruelty,
the human touch.

The sea
left the wound bleeding off-color.
The heron and I

tread time with oceans everywhere,
each step, hesitant, and seeming
to stand on nothing.

Of Grace

catalpa leaves
swell with rain
breathe color
over grass and garden

yellow essence
over bark bones
feet wrapped
against the cold

along the border
of sidewalk and lawn
going to brass
going to earth

and a red maple
lifts soaking palms
toward my window
offers drink

To Live by Water

is to practice deep breathing
as clouds flex over tousled earth

winds unlace willows and clash the ash leaves
as sparrows burst up

not knowing they will die someday
even under a godly eye

the fire of summer probes a creek where small fish
dart like thoughtless words

frogs rev their voices and listen for the slow
sweep of a heron's foot

when a hawk's shadow flies tying sky
to shore and water   self and other

all four elements visible around this pond
a bead shining on the world's ear

Driving for the Eggs

Ahead of me, a shabby four-door Dodge sedan
Slightly off-balance, as if its wheels don't sit squarely,
Rolls along at fifteen miles below the speed limit,
And the driver's white hair shines briefly as we troll
Under a street lamp, nowhere near a school zone,
With all the time in the world,

Except that I need to get to work.
How long can this go on? I wonder
As we both dither our way into the center lane,
Signals flashing in unison. The Dodge turns and sails genteelly
Into an egg shop's parking lot
While I am trapped by oncoming traffic, my blinker
Repeating its impatience in the darkness.

Con Trail

A full moon shone behind rippled clouds,
a silent con trail drew across night sky.
Blue light threw the trail's long shadow

against a cloud on its solitary stroll.
The moon, slow in its movements, paused,
appreciative, saw the trail and its dark second

diverge and drift apart. Light on the cirrus scales
shifted as if soft fish turned in sky water,
past the two lines of light and shadow,

an illusion of depths overhead like those below
in earth, in sea, temporarily brighter
than the unseen schools of stars.

En la Noche

Unseen   paws of wind try the latch
of glass doors

like mice unafraid of cat's ears   cocked and attentive
as cat paws point toward the sounds

however tiny   and hidden
by winter night's creaks and groans

weather leans against our home   its lights sailing in darkness
night and windows gaze into one another's eyes

we listen to the tapping   until it stops

Sheba

Sheba's slender legs
stretch like Audrey Hepburn's gloved arms
held out for her own admiration.

Sheba's button paws step delicately
across the kitchen linoleum
or hinge over the edge of her perch—

the blue blanket folded atop her carrier,
a high spot below a heat duct.
Her round dark head down,

one ear tips up, a tulip cup
in chocolate. Her tail taps out
her thoughts about my voice

saying her name. I can hardly state
how blue are her eyes, the icy
selfish glare of a winter sky

they can show, or the drowsy drift
of summer afternoon watching itself
at a window, or the blaze of blue

and chatter of her teeth
as she moans her desire to bite
sassy sparrows on a branch.

At night, Sheba walks along my chest—
spiking holes in my skin—
and flops, purring, her tiny exhalations

tickling my chin. Then abruptly she's up,
stalks away and rolls against my leg,
presses me with feline two-step

tipped with a bit of back claws.

Awakened in the dark, later,
I realize I have been edged

toward mid-bed at an angle,
the better to allow
Miss Girl her space

while keeping me close.
I know her hidey-holes
where she disappears during the day,

and love her muffled grunt of surprise
when I peek in, seeking
a glimpse, even though

I know what she looks like.
I want her the way she wants me,
idiosyncratically.

Swimming Pool

Buoys bump my shoulder,
Wavering water leads me
And slops into my mouth
That gapes to gasp.
I am not a good swimmer—
My torso twists too far,
My arms arc sideways,
Calf cramps threaten.
Below, the blue line
Crookedly crosses my path
And my lane neighbor
In snorkel and flippers
Knocks knees with me.
Can one stagger in water?

But the clock crawls on,
And somehow this sliding
Continues, calms,
I side-stroke toward my goal,
The top of my skull
Pointing the way,
I lean into the weight
Of weary arms,
Two more, two more,
The count that counts.

Triumph

Triumph has a sweet voice
And eyes the shade of violets

Bright, but half-hidden
By leaves plentiful as tears.

Triumph sails over the lawn
Turning on one small anchor

As do dandelion seeds,
Gossamer insects,

And silver threads lost
From everyday garments

Or a down feather
Fallen from a nest,

No longer needed
And free now

To fly in its way
As we do in ours.

I Miss My Life in the Other Dimension

Today I caught a sense of a different house around me,
Six hundred miles from here, with old woodwork
Lovingly polished, and scuff marks at the doorway
To the living room, site of frequent gatherings
Of artists, friends, professors, students,
The guests who reflect my many connections
And who all love me, my smile wrinkles and soft hands.

Old oak trees in the yard would hover, never a branch
To fall, all the astilbe in place, and the gravel driveway
Straight-edged, not kicked askew into hearty grass,
Deep-rooted in black farmland earth. It's a small town,
So traffic is quiet, and my neighbors wave,
Knowing me a little eccentric but talented.
They read my books, have my art photos mounted.

I must have on the tan cardigan with low pockets
That I can slip my hands into without slumping.
I must be watching jays through a picture window,
Coffee mug fragrant in my palm. Surely a scent
Of baking lingers in sun rays across floorboards.

But the only truth is a brush of cat fur at my ankle
As I work alone, back aching, shivering and stiff
In a room full of things that need dusting
If I ever had time.

Spring Cleaning

Woodchucks knock against rococo ceilings. They've missed
the silver-buckled ride of winter weather
that kicks up the marsh in hard chunks.
Their thigh-hinges are hollow as chaps on a chair.

Unlocked water has disturbed them
in this month that takes their name as a joke. The yard soaks
in spume as from a sleeper's pillow, and the sky's blankets
sag, rinsed sweet after dreams.

A riot of ferns is like the green unfurling
of winter rags dried in knots, sodden in ooze
between the oaks' arthritic toes.
Little fur coats bound across the lawn.

Everything's coming out, in wrinkled finery,
rinsing the pane I look through in sloppy joy.

Trees in Memory

With the trees cut down, suddenly
the front yard yawns with brash sunshine
and sandpapery tips of the mown lawn
show dun-dry, the stems of grass pale

and thirsty for unfamiliar blue.
Maroon bark and leaves litter the sidewalk,
sawdust from the wood chipper
fills each breath. The trucks drive off.

Still in shock—the yard, the birds, the air
gather themselves for a moment before
a scold starts up with sharp pips on the roof:
how could you, how, how, how this?

The Tree Surgeon Dreams of Bowling

Up in the highest joint that holds my weight
against shifting breezes, I dance my hips
while keeping both feet planted, one on a limb,
the other in the crevice of an old scar.
Twigs with fiveleaf fingers stroke
my cheek, then slap when I lift
the cutting tool and let it bite.

That tree-hand falls away, and I look up
into fresh light, release the safety, let
the blade-buzz decrescendo
like applause fading. I seem to be standing
at the line, one arm cocked back and heavy
gripping my favorite bowling ball,
the one marbled with iridescent green,
its old surface chipped
from years of small-town teams

rolling in on Thursday nights,
thirty frames or so, grinding the tiny pencil
to write a 7, an 8, a 6, an X now and then.
But here, in this aging pear tree, my legs splayed wide,
my arm aches from the tool's vibrations—
going nowhere but cutting away
things I wish I didn't need.

ABOUT THE AUTHOR

Jayne Marek's poems and art photos appear in publications such as *The Cortland Review, Amsterdam Quarterly, Women's Studies Quarterly, Notre Dame Review, Raven Chronicles, Spillway, 3Elements, Sliver of Stone, Camas, Gravel, Cold Mountain Review, New Mexico Review, Pontoon Poetry,* and elsewhere. She has provided color cover art for *Silk Road, Bombay Gin,* and *The Bend.* Her prior collections are *Company of Women: New and Selected Poems* (co-authored with Lylanne Musselman and Mary Sexson, 2013), *Imposition of Form on the Natural World* (2013), and *In and Out of Rough Water* (2017). She was a finalist for the Ex Ophidia Press Poetry Prize, the David Martinson–Meadowhawk Prize, and the Ryan R. Gibbs Photography Contest; she has received two fellowships from the National Endowment for the Humanities for literary scholarship and two Pushcart Prize nominations for poetry. Her one-act play "Katherine and Virginia," which characterizes the friendship between authors Katherine Mansfield and Virginia Woolf, has been performed in New York City and Indiana. A professor emerita of English (Ph.D. University of Wisconsin) who also holds an M.F.A. (the University of Notre Dame), she now makes her home in the Pacific Northwest, near the wild and beautiful coast, where she writes, photographs, and learns about natural history.

www.ingramcontent.com/pod-product-compliance
Lightning Source LLC
Chambersburg PA
CBHW021159090426

42740CB00008B/1152